WOODWORKING PROJECTS
✳✳✳FOR YOUR GARDEN AND PORCH✳✳✳

Visit our website at www.skyhorsepublishing.com.

10 9 8 7 6 5 4 3 2 1

Library of Congress Cataloging-in-Publication Data is available on file.

Photos by Malin Nuhma
Cover photos by Malin Nuhma

Print ISBN: 978-1-5107-5899-5
Ebook ISBN: 978-1-5107-0909-6

Printed in China

MATTIAS WENBLAD ✳ PHOTOGRAPHS BY MALIN NUHMA

WOODWORKING PROJECTS

✳✳✳ FOR YOUR GARDEN AND PORCH ✳✳✳

SIMPLE, FUNCTIONAL, AND RUSTIC DÉCOR YOU CAN BUILD YOURSELF

TRANSLATION BY GUN PENHOAT

Skyhorse Publishing

INTRODUCTION

When I was asked to collaborate on a book about woodworking with my wife, who is a photographer, how could I refuse? After all, I have a professional career building Sweden's most beautiful sailboats in a traditional shipyard. My wife and I live in an old house with a beautiful garden. The household has grown along with our family, thanks to two separate additions—our children. Most of the work—both on the interior and exterior of the house—we did ourselves.

Our outdoor space is like a second living room to us; we spend a lot of time working in it and fixing things around the house and the garden. It feels great to share our ideas and projects.

This book should not be taken as an exact how-to manual for building things, but more as a source of inspiration. I want you to generate your own ideas so that you can begin making your own projects. I've included simple illustrations for the larger items, but don't get bogged down by them. Instead, let your own imagination shine. Change, improve, or adapt your work so that it fits you and your home.

Due to this book's somewhat informal style, the descriptions of the projects do not contain pictures or exact step-by-step guidance. We feel that it would be best if you had some prior woodworking experience before starting out, but you shouldn't feel hindered if you have none. Start simply and move on to more challenging projects, at your own pace, as you learn and become more comfortable with the work.

For most of these projects, I've tried to make use of relatively inexpensive materials, so it doesn't really matter if a project doesn't turn out as planned or you end up having to redo something to get it right. The material you use will depend on what you want to build and how much you want to spend. If you opt for lower-cost materials, such as construction/framing grade lumber or different kinds of boards, you'll have to spend a bit more time in the lumberyard to find straight and dry lumber of decent quality. The surface may also be rougher and might require additional planing and sanding to finish it. On the other hand, higher-grade lumber is typically straight, has fewer knotholes, and is often planed and smooth. In this book, I used common construction lumber and planks to build the outdoor mini-kitchen island and the flower box. However, the porch swing and chandelier are both made from planed, pricier wood.

Woodworking is a very meditative occupation for me; it's a wonderful way to tune out everyday problems and let my creativity flow. My hope is that you too will be inspired to get out your tools and start building.

Mattias Wenblad

OUTDOOR MINI-KITCHEN ISLAND

Children love to splash and play with water, so a mini-kitchen island where they're free to let their imagination run wild is perfect for the garden. This island features a concrete work surface that's water-repellent. A plastic tub is repurposed here as sink. See the plan with measurements on p. 101.

A. To make the kitchen island's frame, join the long pieces of lumber with screws.

B. Attach the short pieces with screws to make a "box."

C. The back is anchored by attaching screws on the upper board at the back of the box. You can add a small shelf with brackets onto the back too; it's always nice to have a shelf above the sink for clean dishes and other miscellaneous items.

D. Screw on the planks for the bottom shelf.

E. Now it's time to make the mold for casting the concrete work surface. I like to use shuttering plywood for my mold. Saw pieces to make a small, shallow box. I used the same kind of tub that will be used later to make the

tub hole in the concrete, and cut off its upper rim. The tub is secured by weighing it down with a few stones and a simple cross inside the mold—the tub must not move when the concrete is poured into the mold.

F. Mix the concrete according to the instructions on the bag. Pour the concrete into your mold and spread it out evenly, tapping on the underside with a hammer to remove any air bubbles from the concrete.

I also added a few bolts to the underside of the work surface during casting. The bolts will be used to anchor the surface into the frame once the concrete has cured. The wooden frame has to be treated before the work surface is attached. We opted for a red kitchen island to make a bright and colorful addition to the garden.

PLANTER BOX

It's always such a pleasure to be able to pick homegrown vegetables and herbs for cooking. So, we decided to build a raised planter box; that way it can be easily moved around in the garden depending on where the sun is or where you're cooking. This box works well on a balcony, too. See the plan with measurements on p. 100.

A. I start by assembling the bottom of the box, which consists of a frame made from lumber posts and wooden planks.

B. The box's long sides are made up of two planks that are joined with screws to two short pieces of lumber at each end on what will become the inside of the box. The box's legs are attached with screws to the outside of the long sides. The legs at the back are longer and project over the top; that's where the herb box will later be attached with screws.

C. Once the long side of the box with the legs are ready, the bottom of the box is attached to the long and short sides of the box with screws to form the whole box.

D. The small herb box is screwed onto the top of the longer legs that are attached to the back of the bigger box. Drill a few large draining holes in the bottom of the box.

Treat the surfaces—I stained and oiled the entire structure.

LONG TABLE

A long table in the garden is never out of place. It is always useful, whether as a dining table for a family meal or a coffee table for tea with the neighbors. Here, I built a rustic-looking table with framing lumber. The length of your table is up to you, so feel free to adapt it to your specific needs. You'll find the plan with measurements on p. 101.

A–D. Start by building the legs, which consist of two lumber upright posts with an inserted crosspiece. Mark the area where the crosspiece is to go onto the legs. With a saw, remove a section from the legs corresponding to the crosspiece's thickness and width. The crosspiece is mounted with glue and a bolt made from a piece of dowel. When the glue has dried, saw off the part of the dowel that juts out.

E–F. The tabletop is made from several pieces of board that are glued together, We also mount a strip of lumber to make an edging/frame. Make sure that you have a lot of clamps on hand when gluing the tabletop together and that you're also working on a level surface to prevent the top from becoming warped or twisted.

G. With a miter saw, cut the corners of the edging/frame strips at a 45-degree angle and glue the edging in place. A nail gun is useful to fasten the edges while the glue sets.

CONTINUED ON THE NEXT PAGE.

H–I. Attach the legs with screws. Then fasten, also with screws, a board length-wise between the two crossbars.

J–K. Along the tabletop's edging, mill a profile with the wood router; this is simply to add a decorative touch.

L. After sanding, the whole table is painted with a base coat and then with a topcoat.

SERVING TRAY

A sturdy serving tray is an everyday necessity. This is simple and quick to put together.

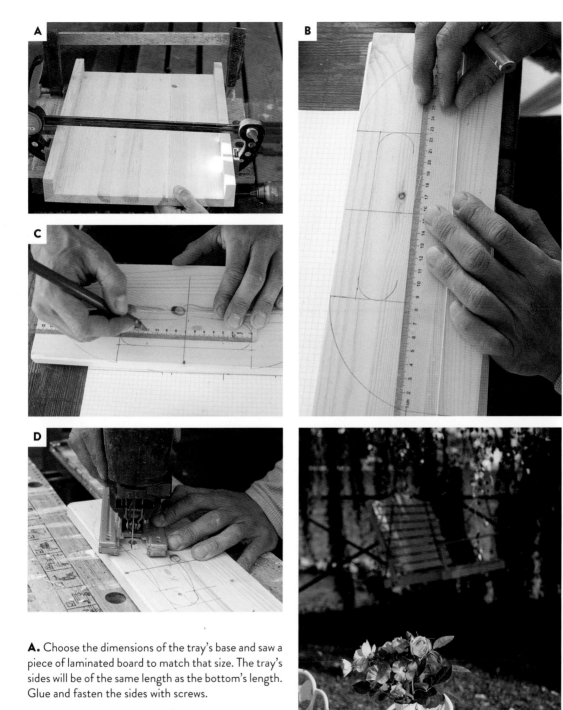

A. Choose the dimensions of the tray's base and saw a piece of laminated board to match that size. The tray's sides will be of the same length as the bottom's length. Glue and fasten the sides with screws.

B–D. The tray's short sides get handles and a more rounded profile. Start by drawing the desired shape onto the board. To cut out the handles, first drill a hole so you're able to insert the jigsaw blade.

Attach the short sides the same way you would the long ones—with glue and screws. Remember to drill first if you're adding a screw near a cut end; this will prevent the wood from splitting. Sand the tray, and paint it in the color of your choice.

GREENHOUSE WALL SHELF

A shelf on which to grow herbs is a useful addition to our newly built greenhouse (you can find out how we built it on p. 93–97). Since the greenhouse itself isn't very roomy, we have to maximize the use of all available space. Instead of just taking a board and adding a few brackets, we made the shelf a bit fancier by adding a gingerbread trim with the saw.

A. Saw the shelf board to the desired length. Draw the pattern you want for the edging. I used a coffee cup as a guide to trace a simple scalloped pattern. Saw the shape with a jigsaw and sand off all the rough edges.

B. Use a miter saw to make handsome-looking corners. This requires a bit of measuring, but once it's done the finish will look polished and professional.

C. The edges are glued on and attached with a nail gun. You can also simply glue the edges on and secure them with clamps until the glue has set.

Lastly, treat the surface. I chose to paint the shelf white.

HAMMOCK STAND

What bliss it is to stretch out in a hammock and enjoy a peaceful swing! Unfortunately, there aren't always trees available or suitable for hanging a hammock, so one solution is to build a hammock stand that can be placed on the ground in the garden. This allows you to position your hammock wherever you want it and makes it simple to move your hammock if you want some shade for a while. See the plan and measurements on p. 103.

A–C. Start by screwing together two long boards; add a few blocks between the pieces. Attach two sturdy lifting eye bolts to the end blocks.

D–E. With a piece of threaded rod and bolts, mount two cross boards to prevent the stand from toppling over.

F. Saw two pieces of board that you will use to hang the hammock. Attach a lifting eye bolt to the end of each piece of board—this is where the hammock will be secured. Attach another lifting eye bolt to the underside of the piece of board, level with the bolt on the board resting on the ground. Hook a length of chain between the two bolts. The chain will prevent the stand from folding when you lie down in the hammock.

PORCH SWING

A summer's dream is a swing hanging from a tree, or perhaps out on the porch, for a leisurely swing on a sunny summer afternoon. See the plan and measurements on p. 102.

A. With a saw, cut out all the pieces for the swing. I add some gingerbread trim with the jigsaw on the top plank of the backrest.

B. Apply a base coat and then the topcoat. It is always easier to paint the pieces before assembling them.

C–D. Using screws, assemble the frame for the seat. Remember that the slats must have an overhang because that is where the hanging mechanism will be attached. Screw on another crosspiece in the middle of the seat to add stability and strength to the slats. Then, fasten the slats one by one with screws.

CONTINUED ON THE NEXT PAGE.

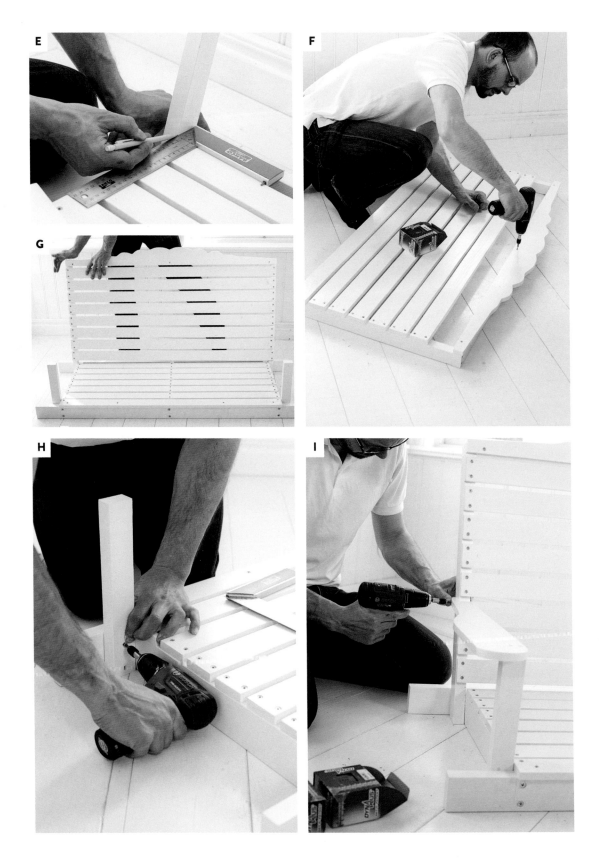

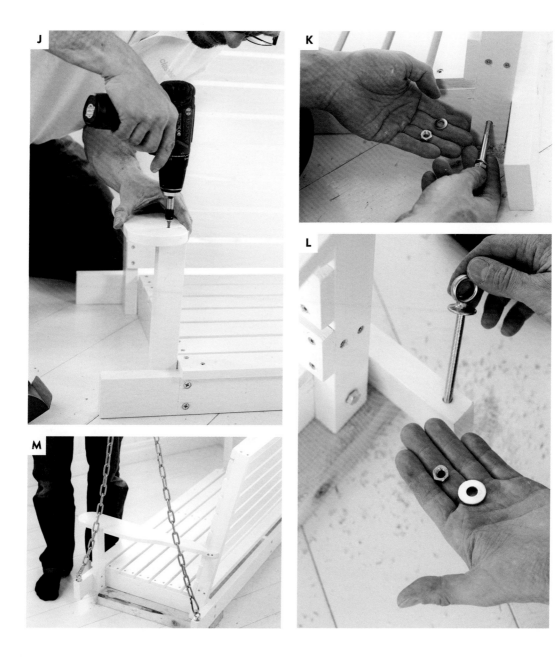

E–G. The backrest is built in the same way as the seat, but the upright pieces will jut downward below the seat to enable you to fasten the seat and back pieces together with screws.

H. Attach the upright pieces on the front of the seat frame with screws. That's where the arm rests will be attached.

I. Attach the backrest to the seat frame.

J. Attach the arm rests to the front upright piece and the backrest.

K–L. Now add the swing attachment: Drill holes for lag eye bolts on the front and back piece of each of the frame's short sides. Attach the eye bolts.

M. Measure and cut the chains to the desired length with an angle grinder. Fasten the chain in the eye bolts with carabiners.

HOBBY HORSE

A three-year-old bursting with energy and imagination needs a hobby horse! Now she can ride off to wild adventures in the big garden.

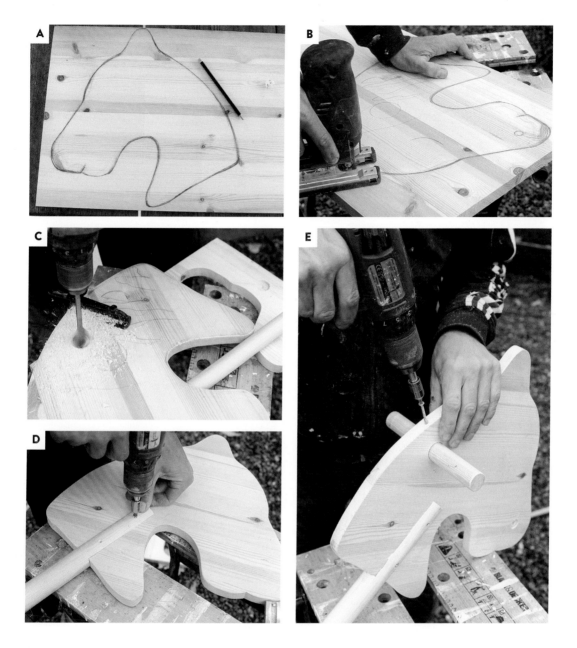

A. Draw the horse's head on a piece of edge-glued pine panel.

B. Cut out the shape of the head with a jigsaw. Sand down all the rough edges.

C. Cut a hole for the handle with an auger drill with the right sized spoon bit. Also, drill the panel surface slightly—just small dents—to make nostrils for the horse.

D. The "body" of the horse is made from a piece of sturdy dowel. Saw a groove in the dowel as thick as the panel, so you can slide on the horse head. Attach the head with screws on both sides.

E. Push the piece of dowel for the handle through the hole. I blocked the handle with a screw to prevent it from coming loose.

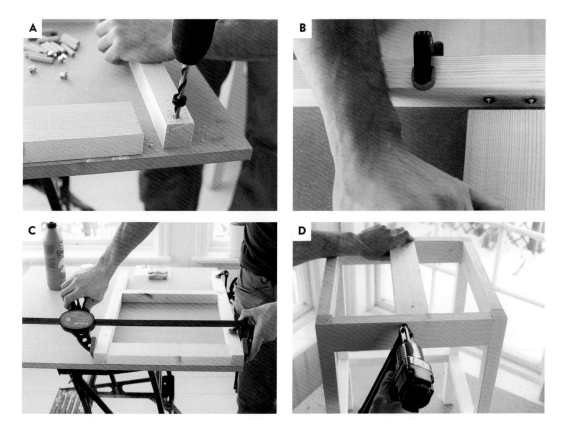

TABLE WITH PATTERNED CONCRETE SLAB

This small table is ideal for your Sunday coffee break. I built the entire frame with glue and butt joints. This is not necessary, of course, but it is a lot of fun. If you'd rather work with butt joints instead of screws, there are sets with drill and dowel markers available for purchase. You'll find the plan and measurements on p. 105.

Start by cutting out the pieces for the frame. Mark where the short sides are to be attached on the legs.

A. Using the drill from the set, cut holes in the legs, making them slightly deeper than half the butt's length.

B. Place the dowel markers (from the drill set) into the drilled holes and press the short sides' ends against the marker points so they mark where you have to drill for the butts. If at all possible, work on a flat and smooth surface as this will make it easier to get everything to fall exactly into place.

Drill into where the short side's marking is, drilling slightly deeper than half the butt's length.

C. Apply glue in the holes and on the end of the board. Attach one side at a time, and secure them with clamps until the glue has set.

D. Once two sides are finished, it's time to piece together the rest of the frame using the same method. Once that's done, attach a piece of leftover lumber between the short ends so you can attach the concrete surface with screws later on.

When the frame is assembled and the glue has dried, sand off all the rough edges with a sanding block and 120-grit sandpaper. Give the frame and the shelf slats a base coat and then a topcoat. The slats will be attached later on.

CONTINUED ON THE NEXT PAGE.

E. While the paint is drying, cut out the pieces for the casting mold. I use special plywood—shuttering plywood—that is commonly used for casting concrete. We decided to add paper with a raised design to the bottom of the mold; this will become the surface of the concrete and will feature a nice pattern once the concrete has cured. Use the nail gun to put together the mold.

Mix the concrete (such as Quikrete) according to the instructions. Make sure that the concrete is not too firm or it won't spread easily.

F. Pour in half of the concrete, add some concrete mesh reinforcement, and fill to the top of the mold with the remaining concrete. Tap the mold with a hammer to make the concrete spread out and to remove any air bubbles.

G. Attach two bolts into the concrete. Later on they will be used to attach the concrete slab to the frame. You can hang the bolts in the concrete before it dries. Hang them from a piece of scrap lumber where you've made holes for the bolts.

H. Once the paint has dried, assemble the slats for the shelf with glue and a nail gun. We turned the table upside-down for an easier reach when using the nail gun. You can also screw down the slats from underneath to conceal the screw heads.

Sand the concrete slab's edges with a random orbital sander using 80-grit sandpaper. Treat the surface of the concrete slab with tung oil. Attach the slab to the table.

STORYTELLER'S BENCH

In the lingering dusk of a summer's eve, you should have a bench where you can sit and spin yarns. The tales you tell may grow a bit tall, but it hardly matters when the sun is slowly disappearing over the horizon. . . . See the plan and measurements on p. 103.

I built this bench from inexpensive construction lumber. Saw the seating planks to the length you need.

A. Attach two cross bars underneath the seating planks with screws.

B. The legs are made up of two X's, where one piece is sunken into the other. Place the leg pieces on top of each other to make an X, and outline both top pieces on the bottom ones so you know how much you have to cut away.

C. Use a handsaw when you cut the lines to ensure that you get a straight and correct cut. Saw down to half the depth of the leg piece. The rest is cut with a circular saw so you can adjust the depth of the cut. Glue and screw together the legs. Push the pieces together so you end up with an almost level X. The legs are attached to the crossbars under the seat, with screws.

I made the small table from two pieces of board screwed together to make a T. I made a groove in the lower bit of the upright piece, so the T can be slid onto the bench and attached with a screw.

D. Treat the surface to suit your preference; here I used a black stain for outdoor use.

SOAPBOX CAR

- - - - - - - - - - - - - - - - - -

Most kids love a great soapbox car, but the grownups having to play the part of the engine—not so much. So when the adults get tired of the game, kids quickly learn to ride around with each other in this car. See the plan and measurements on p. 104.

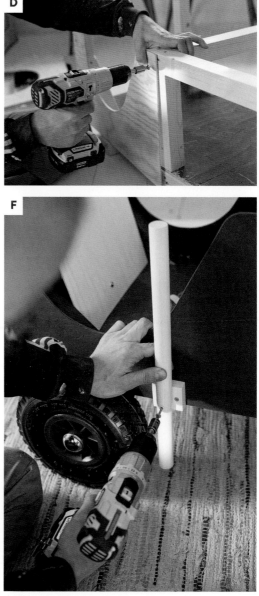

Cut the pieces for the frame according to the plan on p. 104.

A–B. Start by assembling the undercarriage. Attach the board (which will become the floor of the car) to the undercarriage. Then put together the rest of the frame.

C. Attach the piece of lumber for the back wheels and the other piece of lumber for the front wheels. The piece for the front wheels is attached with bolts, washers, and locknuts. This will allow the wheels to turn once you've finished.

D. Cut out the pieces for the car's body with your saw, and mount them. Once that's done, sand all the rough edges. Now it's time to paint the car in the color of your choice. I made a template and painted numbers on the hood. We'll put together some rear lights and the grille with leftover pieces of plywood. Two metal lids from old canning jars will become headlights.

E. I purchased a car kit with tires and wheel axles. Assemble the wheels according to the instructions. Now attach them to the pieces of lumber for the wheels under the car. Drill holes in the front axle for the wheels. Attach a sturdy length of rope that will work for steering.

F. A piece of dowel becomes the brake for one of the back wheels.

DRIFTWOOD SHELF

A few old planks of driftwood we had picked up at a beach on the West Coast turn into a great little shelf.

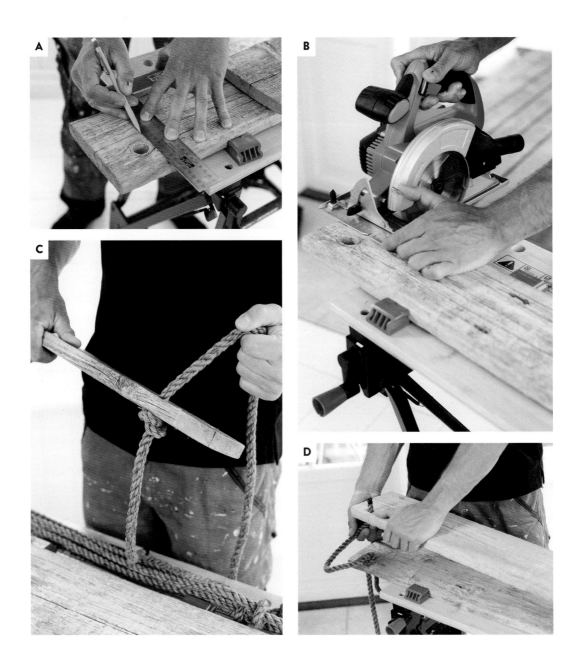

A. Measure the length of the planks that are going to be used as the shelf's surface.

B. Cut the planks to the same size and level right to the ends. Mark where the holes for the attached cords will be, and drill the holes.

C–D. Pull the cord through the holes and secure the shelf with sailors' knots under each shelf.

CONCRETE PAVERS

Concrete is a fun and inexpensive material to work with, and you can make lots of handy things for the garden with it: bird baths, pots, bench slabs, garden pavers . . . I tried it out by making a patterned concrete paver that fits in front of the entrance to the greenhouse.

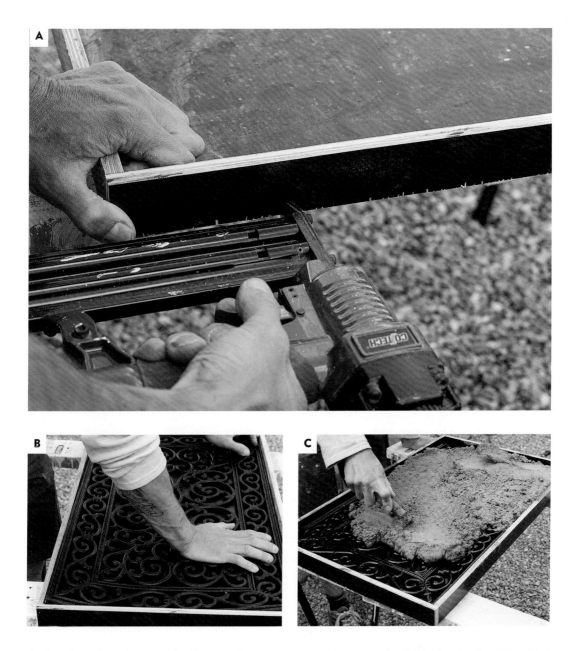

A. Start by making the mold. I build it with shuttering plywood—special plywood used for casting concrete. With a saw, cut out the bottom to the size you want. Cut guiding strips to use for the sides, too. I made our paver just over an inch (3 cm) thick, which means that the strips need to be that wide too, plus the thickness of the paver. Assemble the mold with nails or screws.

B. I used a rubber doormat as a pattern. Place it in the bottom of the mold. It's best to brush it lightly with some cooking oil to make it easier to remove once the concrete has finished curing (i.e., it has dried and hardened). Mix the concrete according to the instructions on the bag.

C. Pour the concrete until the mold is half full. Spread it evenly with a trowel and tap it with a hammer to remove any air bubbles. Tapping on the underside and the sides should remove the air bubbles.

CONTINUED ON THE NEXT PAGE.

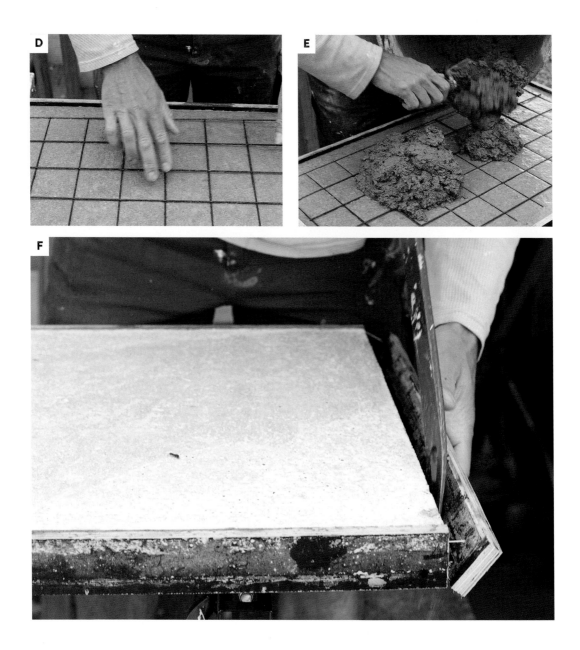

D-E. Now add the concrete mesh reinforcement, which is cut slightly smaller than the mold. Pour in the rest of the concrete so the mold is full. Tap to remove any air bubbles, and make sure the mold is standing on a level surface or the paver will come out unevenly thick.

F. You should spray the concrete with water within the first 24 hours, and cover the mold with a sheet of plastic to lessen the risk of the paver cracking. After about 24 to 48 hours, once the concrete has "cured" and is dry and solid, it's time to break off the mold and pull off the doormat.

POTTING BENCH

If you've ever built a greenhouse, you need somewhere to grow things. You can do that either in pots or directly in the soil. However, I really wanted a potting bench that could also be used as seating. After all, you need to sit somewhere, too!

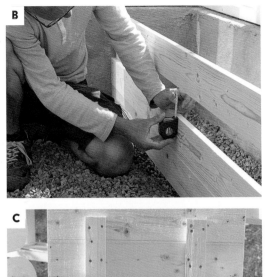

A. Start by attaching two upright posts directly onto the wall at each end of the greenhouse.

B. Attach planks with screws to the upright posts to make a low wall. Add a short perpendicular wall in between to separate and stabilize the construction.

C. Build the lid to the bench from the same type of planks used for the wall, adding two planks to the underside of the lid to hold it all together.

D. I also built a simple backrest that is attached to

the greenhouse's framing structure. It makes for more comfortable seating, and you don't need to use the windows as a backrest. I rounded the backrest's planks with the jigsaw so they look like big popsicle sticks.

E. Cut out two pieces of lumber with a light slant to give the backrest a more comfortable angle. Attach the backrest planks with screws. Finally, treat the surface of the bench; I covered mine with a white-tinted stain.

COLD FRAME

It's not a bad idea to have a small cold frame in the yard; the window lets the temperature rise on the inside so it can extend your growing season into spring and fall. Perhaps you can place it near the kitchen to grow herbs and spices—it's a real perk to have fresh seasonings on hand when cooking. See the plan and measurements on p. 101.

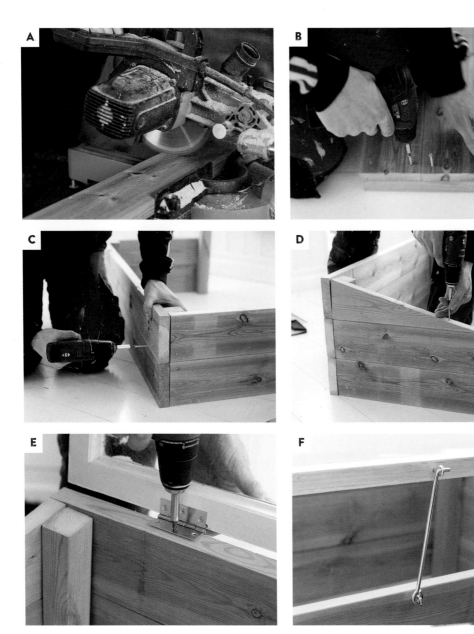

Start off with an old window, perhaps one stored up in the attic or a cheap one found at a yard sale. Since you'll be using the window as a lid, use its measurements as a guide to build the rest of your cold frame. The measurements here are adapted to the window I had on hand.

A. Using a saw, start by cutting the required pieces following the plan: planks for the cold frame's long and short sides, two pieces of upright posts twice the height of the plank, and two posts three times the height of the plank.

B. Attach the long sides to the upright posts with screws. The back of the box is taller by one plank's width.

C–D. Attach the short sides with screws and also the angle cut pieces.

E. Now, mount the window and hinges.

F. Attach a window stay to the front so you can leave the window propped open.

GATELEG TABLE

....

In the greenhouse, we need a table that's
adjustable so we can use it for different
tasks. That's why I decided to build a
small gateleg table that will be useful in a
variety of settings. You'll find the plan and
measurements on p. 103.

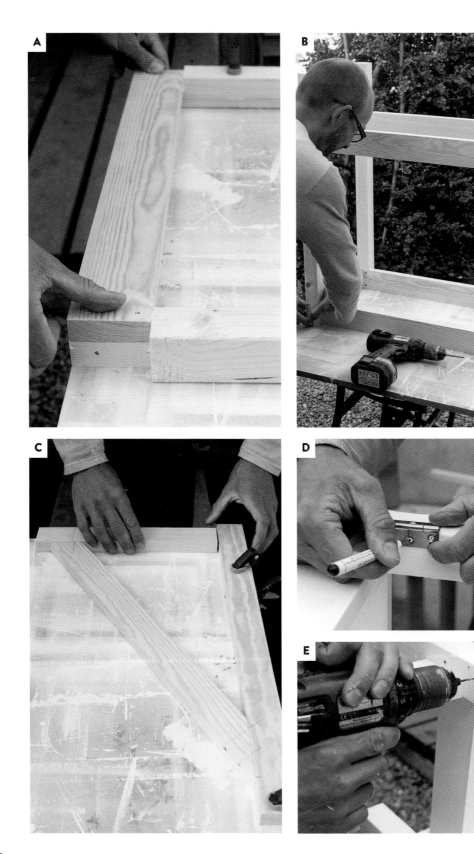

A. Start by sawing the legs and the crossbars that will hold the leg construction together. The crossbars are fitted into a notch in the legs where wood—the width and the thickness of the crossbar—has been cut out.

B. Assemble the entire leg construction with screws.

C. Continue with the triangles that support the table's leaves (which can be folded up and down). Glue the triangles and secure with screws.

D–F. Once the table's leg construction is painted, it's time to attach the support triangles. They're situated

approximately ⅛ inch (a few millimeters) below the tabletop's underside. This is so they're easy to fold aside when the leaves need to be turned down. The support triangles are attached with hinges.

G. The tabletop has three leaves that are joined with hinges. Screw and glue down the middle part of the tabletop onto the leg construction.

H. Finally, add small wood blocks at the ends of the triangles supporting the folding leaves.

CURVED SOFA

Inspired by the soft, curved cliffs of the Bohus coast in Sweden, I got the idea to build a comfortable sofa, a place to sit while enjoying a drink at dusk or while reading the newspaper on a quiet summer's morning. See the plan and measurements on p. 105.

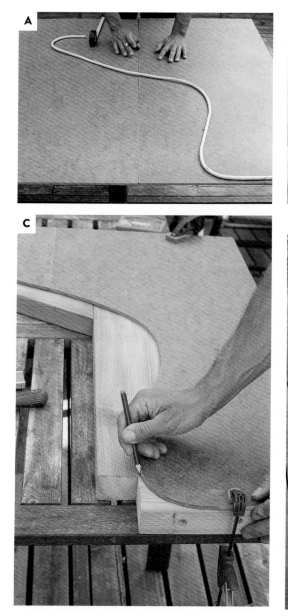

A. To achieve the shape of the sofa, I used a piece of Masonite hardboard and a flexible electric cable. Draw the form you want and cut it out with the jigsaw—this will be your template.

B. Cut your lumber so that it fits your template. You will have to try different ways until you find all the desired lengths and angles. Then, simply assemble the frame by screwing it together. However, be careful so you don't place the screws where you're going to have to make cuts later on.

C. Place the Masonite template onto the frame and trace the shape. Cut out the shape with a saw. I made three frames for our sofa. Cut all the needed slats. Treat the surface of the slats and the frame before you assemble them.

D. Now you just have to attach the slats by screwing them onto the frame.

OTTOMAN/ SOFA TABLE

The construction method used for this project is the same as the one used for the sofa above (p. 62). Here, though, you'll only need to join two pieces for the frame for the ottoman, and only two frames are needed. Draw the design you want onto the frame pieces, and cut them with the jigsaw. Then you just have to attach the slats.

WORK TABLE

This is a potting station for the garden. When you work in the yard, you always need a work surface where you can go about your planting as well as prepare and look after your plants. It's a great area to muck around with the soil, and it's handy to have a place to store your tools and miscellaneous garden accessories. The plan with measurements is on p. 105.

Using a saw, start by cutting out all the pieces for the frame, following the plan drawing.

A. Screw on the edging for the long side on two legs, and then attach it on the short sides. The screw heads will be visible, so be extra careful to measure out the space and pre-drill so that the screws' placements look nice and symmetrical.

B. Now it's time to start on the shelf. Assemble the frame with screws. This shelf is then mounted onto the table legs—a few clamps will help hold the frame in place while you screw it down. Mark and pre-drill for the screws that you're going to fasten the slats with.

C. Attach the shelf slats. Leave a small space between the slats so that water can run off. Sand all the rough edges with a sanding block and fine grit sandpaper.

Treat the surface of the table with a solution of ferrous sulfate or a pigmented oil stain, as this will protect the wood and give it a nice patina over time.

D. It's now time to make the frame for the welded mesh reinforcement we're going to use for the back. Assemble the frame with screws, and mount the mesh on the back of the frame. Use heavy duty metal shears to cut the wire mesh to fit your frame.

CONTINUED ON THE NEXT PAGE.

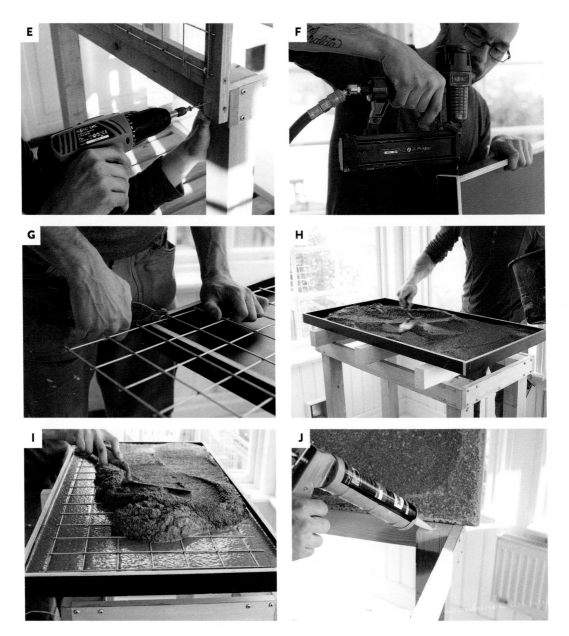

E. Attach the mesh frame with screws in the table construction's edging. You can make the frame rectangular or you can let the short sides protrude slightly to facilitate the fastening.

F. Build the mold for the concrete surface: with a saw, cut out the pieces for the mold. I used shuttering plywood, which is special plywood used for casting concrete. Assemble the mold with a nail gun.

G. Cut out a piece of welded mesh reinforcement slightly smaller than the mold.

H. Mix the concrete according to the instructions on the bag. Fill the mold half full. Using a hammer, tap underneath to remove any air bubbles.

I. Place the mesh reinforcement into the mold, and then fill the rest of the mold with concrete. Tap again to remove any air bubbles.

J. Once the concrete slab has cured, mount it with heavy-duty construction glue.

CHANDELIER

It's a great idea to hang a chandelier out on the porch or in the greenhouse, especially for those of us who like to use our outdoor spaces late into the season. Setting a nice dinner table in the greenhouse in late September, lit by candlelight, adds a nice touch to everyday living.

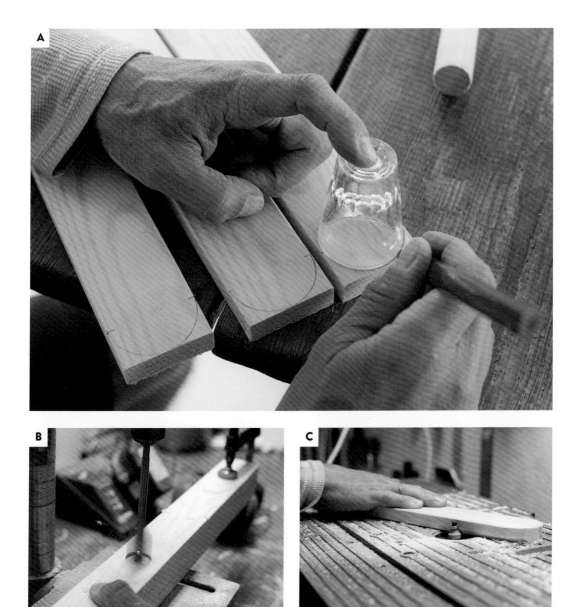

A. Select three narrow planks and cut them to the same length—they will make the chandelier's arms. Cut a piece of strong dowel to the desired length for the middle piece. I traced the ends of the planks, with the help of a small glass, to impart a soft shape to the arms. Cut them with the jigsaw.

B. Measure to find the center on the planks, and drill a hole of the same diameter as the dowel.

C. I also milled a simple profile with the router along the edges. This is not strictly necessary, but it adds a decorative detail.

CONTINUED ON THE NEXT PAGE.

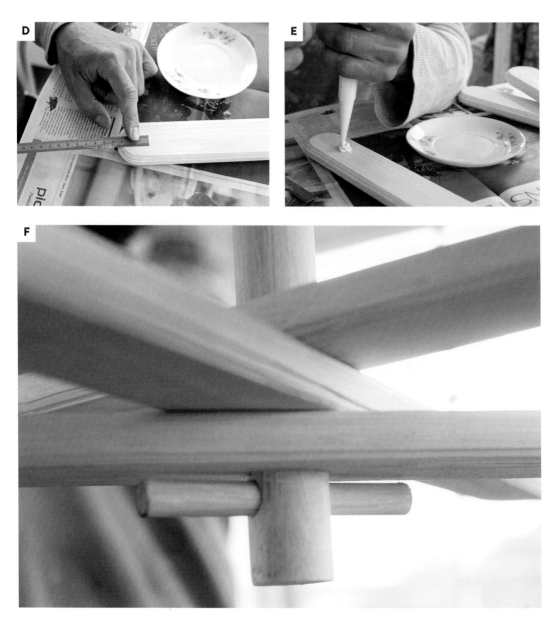

D–E. After treating the surface of the pieces—I chose to paint them white—measure where to set the candleholders. With a crayon, mark those spots for the glue. I used Sikaflex Fast to attach six small saucers, which will become candleholders at the end of each arm.

F. Slide the arms onto the big dowel when the Sikaflex Fast has cured, and block the arms with a smaller dowel further down where you have drilled a hole.

Add a hook at the top of the big dowel to hang the chandelier.

GREENHOUSE
CUPBOARD

I think that a cupboard for storing odds and
ends—a dedicated space to put all those things
that might come in handy—should have a
spot in the new greenhouse. The plan with
measurements is on p. 107.

Start by sawing the planks for the sides and back following the plan measurements on p. 107. I used an old window without glass for the cupboard door. If you have a window, modify the cupboard measurements according to it. If not, make a wood frame. I wanted to paint the planks with the basecoat and also at least one layer of topcoat, since I used slightly thinner tongue and groove floor planks. If not, I might have ended up with a stripy-looking cupboard because the wood could move and separate a little.

A. Attach the sides and the back to the bottom and top parts so you get a big box.

B. Cut the legs from some framing lumber, and glue and screw them in place.

C Glue and nail a wood strip to the inside of the cupboard to reinforce the sides. This also adds more material to attach the hinges to.

D. Set the window (which will be the door) in its place, and measure for the upper and lower plank pieces that will be fitted onto the front of the cupboard.

E. Now it's time for the supports that will hold the shelves. Glue and nail or screw them to the inside of the cupboard where you want the shelves to be.

F. Paint the entire cupboard, inside and out.

G. Fasten poultry netting to the inside of the window. Then, simply attach the window with the appropriate hinges.

H. I made the shelving out of the same tongue and groove floor planks I used for the cupboard's sides and back.

PLANTER BOXES WITH TRELLIS

Creating different garden rooms makes the yard cozier and more exciting. You can modify and rebuild the garden using moveable room dividers. The plan with measurements is on p. 102.

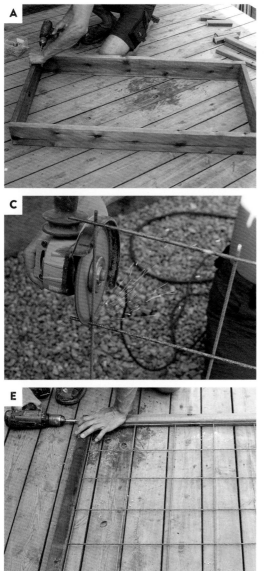

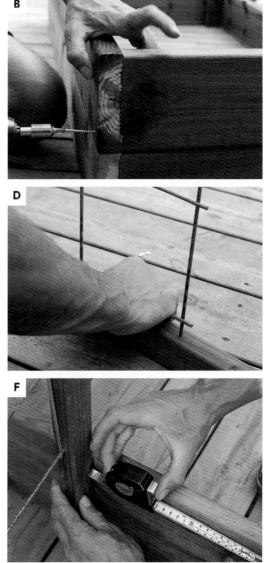

A. With a saw, cut the pieces for the boxes. Screw together the bottom frame.

B. Now screw together the upper frame. The frames are put together with additional short wood corner braces.

C. I built the trellis out of welded mesh reinforcement and lumber. Cut the mesh to the right size. Leave a few of the dangling wires intact on each side, and cut off the rest.

D. Mark on each piece of lumber where the protruding wires are located. Drill holes with a drill bit slightly larger in diameter than the diameter of the mesh wires. These will keep the mesh in place in the frame.

E. Screw together the frame with the mesh inserted into the holes you have drilled.

F. Mount the trellis into the middle of the box; that way you can plant on either side of the trellis.

OUTDOOR KITCHEN ISLAND

It happens to all of us, right? We're in the middle of grilling and we run out of space to set things down. An outdoor kitchen island will make life easier and cookouts even more fun. The plan with measurements is on p. 106.

Cut out the pieces for the frame according to the measurements on the plan. Paint all pieces with a base coat and topcoat.

A. Begin by attaching the short cross planks over the legs (under the work surface) with screws. These are for fastening the work surface to later on. Also, attach the upper board to the short sides.

B. Attach the wheels to the shorter pair of legs.

C. Using screws, assemble the "hold-all" shelf below the work surface. Start with the frame and then, using nails, add the slats for the shelf.

CONTINUED ON THE NEXT PAGE.

D–E. Mount the shelf at the desired height. Use a bit of scrap lumber and four clamps for temporary support while the shelf is being secured. The work will be easier if the island frame is turned upside down and set on an even surface.

F. Continue by attaching the upper board, going along the long sides, to the legs. Remember to check that the legs are parallel—double-check the space between the legs at the top and the bottom.

Now you can apply putty and a final coat of paint. I built the work surface with some leftover planks from the façade of our house.

PLAY TENT

This cubbyhole—or play tent—can double up as a shady spot for younger kids. It might be just the thing for sunny days to crawl into to get away from the hot sun . . . or from mom and dad.

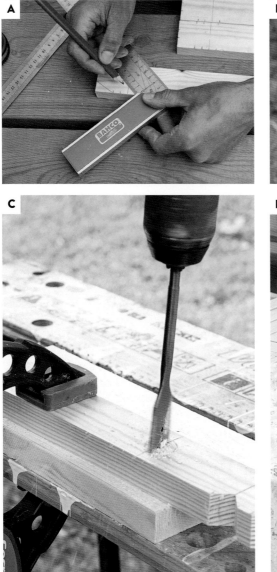

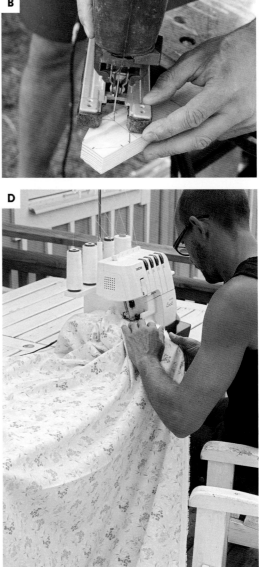

Saw four upright posts of equal length; they will determine the height of the cubbyhole. Then cut three pieces of dowel—these will determine the depth of the cubbyhole.

A–B. I cut some gingerbread trim at the end of the posts—strictly optional, but still fun and decorative.

C. Drill holes for the dowel in the upright posts using a drill bit of the same diameter as the dowel. It's better if you encounter a bit of resistance when pushing the dowel through the posts.

D. Measure and cut out, with seam allowance, a piece of material that will fit the cubbyhole. Hem all the edges and sew pockets along both the short sides for the dowels. You're now ready to pull the material onto the dowels and assemble the cubbyhole.

SWING

A swing is a must if you have small children in the family. It's especially nice once they learn to use the swing by themselves, but it does take a bit of practice.

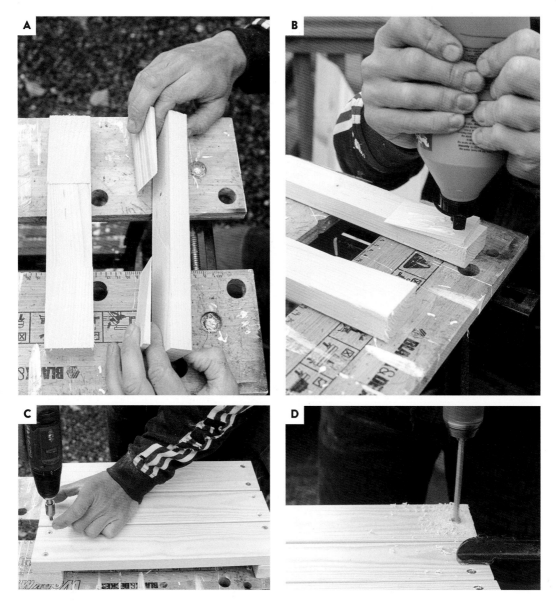

A. Start by cutting out the pieces where the seat will be attached. I sawed a few wedges to give the seat a slight bowl-shape in the middle, which you'll notice in the side-view. That way it's easier to sit securely, as the slight indentation makes it more difficult to slide off.

B. Glue the wedges on, pointing the thickest part towards the end of each bar.

C. Screw down the slats that make up the seat. Sand all the rough edges.

D. Drill holes for the swing's attachment rope.

Push the ropes through the holes and tie sturdy knots under the seat. Test the weight-bearing knots' strength before letting the kids use the swing.

GREENHOUSE

I've always wanted a greenhouse where climbing vines can flourish and where you can sit and enjoy your coffee break when it's a bit too blustery outside. We wanted a classic greenhouse with a foundation wall and white-painted wood. We're finally ready to tackle this project. The plan with measurements is on p. 107.

A. Begin with the foundation. Dig down to solid ground and level the foundation. Make sure that the material you use for your foundation is solidly compacted.

B. Screw together two frames, which will be the mold for the cast concrete girder. Before you start casting, make sure that the frames lie perfectly flat on the ground and that all corners make a precise 90-degree angle. Reinforce the girder with metal mesh; now start mixing and pouring the concrete.

C. When the concrete has cured (when it is dry and hard) it's time to build the foundation wall. The wall consists of two layers of LECA (Light Expanded Clay Aggregate) blocks assembled with mortar. When the wall is finished, give it a "mortar wash," which is done by diluting mortar with some extra water and brushing it over the wall with a sturdy brush. For best results, you might need to repeat this wash up to three times.

D. Place a strip of tarpaper onto the foundation wall before attaching the wooden frame. Measure, saw, and then paint all the boards and edges for the frame twice before starting building.

E. Now it's time to work on the frame. Off to the side, screw together the long walls and lift them into place. Use some scrap lumber for support so nothing falls. Use a laser level to check that the walls are properly aligned.

F. The walls are then mounted to the foundation wall with special LECA block screws.

G. Cut some gingerbread trim on the roof beam where the trusses will be mounted. Once you've decided on the roof's slope, it's time to attach the rafters. Screw down the first four outer rafters. The next step will be to lift the roof, so now is the perfect opportunity to ask for some assistance.

H–I. Using a plumb line, set the whole roof build into the correct position. Once you've checked its alignment, attach it securely. Continue to fasten the rest of the roof rafters; cut and attach them as before.

CONTINUED ON THE NEXT PAGE.

95

J. The short side frame is built in place.

K. Cut down the roof rafters' excess length so you have just enough overhang.

L. A board is screwed onto the ends of the rafters to prevent the glass panes from sliding off.

M–N. Now it's time to attach strips of wood where the glass panes will rest, both on the roof and in the walls. Screw together two small pieces of board to form an L, which you can then use instead of a ruler to attach the wood at equal distances everywhere. It is easier to use than the ruler or yardstick to attach each piece evenly.

O. After the glass panes are in place, another strip of wood is fastened above so the pane can't slide.

P. Build a simple doorframe, check it for correct alignment, and attach it in the doorway.

Q–R. Measure and mark where to set the door hinges. The hinges are sunk into the doorframe. With a chisel, remove enough wood so the hinges fit tightly.

S. Above the door where a triangle-shaped pane of glass should be, I've used common tongue and groove paneling instead, but feel free to install a glass panel if you prefer.